M U S H R O O M S

MUSHROOMS

A Book of Recipes

INTRODUCTION BY SUE LAWRENCE

LORENZ BOOKS
NEW YORK • LONDON • SYDNEY • BATH

This edition published in 1996 by Lorenz Books
an imprint of Anness Publishing Limited
administrative office: 27 West 20th Street
New York, NY 10011

© 1996 Anness Publishing Limited

Lorenz Books are available for bulk purchase for sales promotion and for
premium use. For details write or call the Manager of Special Sales,
Lorenz Books, 27 West 20th Street, New York, NY 10011; (212) 807-6739.

ISBN 1 85967 247 7

Publisher Joanna Lorenz
Senior Cookery Editor Linda Fraser
Cookery Editor Anne Hildyard
Designer Lisa Tai
Illustrations Anna Koska
Photographers Karl Adamson, David Armstrong, Steve Baxter, James Duncan, Michelle Garrett,
Nelson Hargreaves and Amanda Heywood
Recipes Alex Barker, Carla Capalbo, Elizabeth Wolf-Cohen, Shirley Gill, Norma MacMillan, Liz Trigg,
Laura Washburn, Pamela Westland and Steven Wheeler
Food for photography Elizabeth Wolf-Cohen, Carole Handslip, Wendy Lee and Jane Stevenson
Stylists Madeleine Brehaut, Blake Minton and Kirsty Rawlings
Jacket photography Amanda Heywood

Typeset by MC Typeset Ltd, Rochester, Kent
Printed in Singapore by
Star Standard Industries Pte Ltd

Contents

$\mathcal{I}$NTRODUCTION

They like to be kept in the dark. All fungi do. Most of the mushrooms we eat are cultivated ones, which are grown in controlled darkness to keep their pure white color. Wild mushrooms usually grow in dark or shaded woodlands. Until some years ago, we too were kept in the dark about all the different varieties available. It was button mushrooms or nothing for most of us. But now there is a cornucopia of wild and culti-vated mushrooms out there, all ready for the picking.

I have vivid memories of mushroom picking in the woods of north Finland. Here the Finns come out every autumn to pick both mushrooms and berries, to sustain them through the hard winter ahead. The mushrooms are either dried or salted and used in all sorts of savory dishes; from reindeer stews to creamy mush-room pie. Elsewhere in Europe, keen mycologists have trundled out in the autumn to pick the fine offerings of nearby woods. But in North America, it is only recently that we have become aware of the marvelous potential out there. Now we can not only choose from an exten-sive array of cultivated mushrooms, but also from the many varieties of fresh and dried wild ones, many of which are picked in this country. We too are getting the mushroom-picking bug.

There are now cultivated crimini, oyster and shiitake mushrooms

to add to the button mushrooms. Wild ones, such as ceps or morels are often to be seen for sale in good delicatessens or vegetable markets and also on restaurant menus all over the country. Instead of having mushrooms as merely garnish, they are given pride of place. The meaty texture of many types means they make excellent additions to stews, casseroles or sauces. Their affinity with both butter and olive oil means they are also often cooked very simply and served alone, perhaps with a sprinkling of fresh parsley.

In this book, you will also find more innovative dishes: English Muffins with Mushrooms, Tuna Shiitake Teriyaki, Pasta with Mushrooms and Chorizo, for example. But there are also interesting interpreta-tions of the classics, such as Mushroom and Bacon Risotto, Mushroom Macaroni and Cheese, and Spinach and Mushroom Roulade. There are good combinations with fresh herbs – Salmon with Tarragon and Mush-rooms, and Crunchy Mushrooms with Dill Dip.

It would be difficult to find more versatile vegetables than mushrooms; they please carnivores and vegetarians alike. Their role varies: it can both enhance and dominate. The humble mushroom might live its life in the dark, but it certainly brings sunshine to the plate.

Sue Lawrence

Types of Mushroom

SLICED BUTTON MUSHROOMS

The flavor is very mild, and they are good sliced and eaten raw in salads.

CLOSED CUP MUSHROOMS

Good eaten raw or lightly cooked in stir-fries.

OPEN CUP MUSHROOMS

At this stage the brown gills are showing and the cap is darker. Good for stuffing and baking.

FLAT MUSHROOMS

When the cap is quite flat, mushrooms have the best flavor. This makes them ideal for soup.

CANNED BUTTON MUSHROOMS

These make a useful addition to soups, stews, pasta and rice dishes.

SHIITAKE MUSHROOMS

These are of Asian origin and are moist and fleshy with a strong flavor.

OYSTER MUSHROOMS

Moist, delicate pale gray or yellow flesh. They are so named because they are thought to resemble oyster shells.

MORELS

These are intensely perfumed, expensive and beloved of gourmets. They are hard to come by but only a few are needed. Morels are available dried.

BOLETUS, CEPE OR PORCINI

The boletus has a round brown cap and thick stem. It is strongly flavored, and is often dried.

BROWN CAP MUSHROOMS

All-purpose mushrooms with brown caps, also known as *champignons de Paris* or crimini.

PRESERVED MUSHROOMS

Wild varieties are often preserved in oil and sometimes roasted over charcoal first. Good for antipasto.

Preserved mushrooms

Sliced button mushrooms

Yellow oyster mushrooms

Brown cap mushrooms

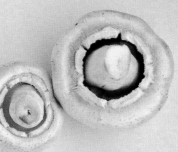
Open cup mushrooms

Button mushrooms

Shiitake mushrooms

Closed cup mushrooms

Dried cèpes

Canned button mushrooms

Dried morels

Flat mushrooms

Preserved mushrooms

Gray oyster mushrooms

Brown cap mushrooms

$\mathscr{B}$ASIC $\mathscr{T}$ECHNIQUES

PREPARING MUSHROOMS

Both cultivated and wild mushrooms will have some soil or sand clinging to them. They absorb water easily and must not be allowed to become waterlogged, however those with deep gills or pockets, such as morels, can be soaked for a few minutes to remove any grit.

Trim the stem ends from wild mushrooms only if they are bruised. Small mushrooms can be left whole; larger ones can be sliced or chopped.

Rinse or wipe mushrooms with a damp cloth or paper towel.

DRYING MUSHROOMS

Drying mushrooms is a method of preservation that causes the essential flavors and aromas to intensify. The dried mushrooms will keep in an airtight jar for many months and can be added to soups and stews.

Wipe the mushrooms with a damp cloth or paper towel and cut away any parts that are damaged or bruised. Using a sharp knife, slice the mushrooms thinly.

Arrange the sliced mushrooms in a single layer on a basket tray or baking sheet lined with newspaper and baking parchment. Put the tray in a warm, airy place for two days.

Place the dried mushrooms in an airtight, clean jar, label and store in a dark place. If the mushrooms are not completely dry, molds may develop in storage. Check them before using.

COOKING MUSHROOMS

Nutritionally, mushrooms contain very little but protein. They are valued for their strong, distinctive flavor and particular chewy texture when cooked. Only the common mushroom can be eaten raw with safety. Cultivated or store-bought wild mushrooms should always be cooked. Because they produce a lot of liquid and shrink in size, mushrooms are best cooked by first lightly sautéeing them in butter or olive oil, which seals in their flavor.

FREEZING MUSHROOMS

Mushrooms can be frozen successfully as they retain their flavor when thawed. Firmer varieties such as shiitake, closed cup and flat mushrooms are suitable candidates for freezing. Thaw them by dropping them briefly into boiling water just before use.

Make sure mushrooms are clean and free from grit and insects. Slice thickly if they are large. Drop them into a pan of boiling salted water for 1 minute. Remove and drain well. Open freeze on a tray for 30–40 minutes. Store them in plastic bags or rigid containers in the freezer for up to six months.

COOK'S TIPS

• *Buying fresh*: Choose mushrooms that are firm and moist but without damp patches or dry stalk ends. Some wild mushroom varieties may have worms; these are not harmful and can be cut away before cooking. To establish if any are present, break off the stems of a few and cut through the caps.

• *Storing fresh*: Mushrooms do not store well if they become wet or sweaty. Store them in a refrigerator in a paper bag or covered with a damp cloth. They keep for up to four days in this way. Clean mushrooms before using in recipes.

• *Dried mushrooms*: These keep indefinitely in an airtight container in a cool place. Before use, soak them in tepid water for 25–30 minutes or add them directly to soups.

PICKLED MUSHROOMS

Pickling mushrooms preserves them as immersing them in vinegar inhibits any bacterial growth. This recipe gives the mushrooms a Chinese flavor, and firm varieties such as shiitake or chestnut mushrooms can be used.

Bring 1 cup white wine vinegar and ⅔ cup water to a boil in a stainless steel pan. Add 1 teaspoon salt, 1 chopped red chili, 2 teaspoons coriander seeds, and 9 ounces firm mushrooms (halved if large) and simmer for ten minutes. Cool.

Sterilize a small preserving jar with boiling water. Drain until dry. Place the mushrooms and their liquid in the jar, seal, label and leave for at least ten days to mature.

MAKING A MUSHROOM GARNISH

Mushrooms make an attractive garnish when they are fluted. To do this you will need to use very fresh white mushrooms and a small, sharp knife. The fluted mushrooms are then rubbed with lemon juice to prevent them from turning brown, or cooked *à blanc* (see right), or they can be sautéed in butter.

Using a small, sharp knife, and holding the blade at an angle, cut away a thin strip from the center to the edge of the cap. Continue in this way evenly around the mushroom, removing the parings. Trim the stem flat.

PRESERVING MUSHROOMS IN OIL

Preserving mushrooms in oil may seem an extravagance, but the following recipe makes a delicious condiment. The oil is so full of flavor it can be used to make salad dressings. It will keep for up to 1 year.

Bring 1 cup white wine vinegar and ⅔ cup water to a boil in a stainless steel pan. Add 1 teaspoon salt, 1 thyme sprig and 1 bay leaf. Infuse for 15 minutes. Add 1 pound assorted mushrooms and simmer for ten minutes.

Lift the mushrooms out of the liquid, drain well and place in a small, sterilized preserving jar.

Cover the mushrooms completely with 1⅔ cups olive oil, cover and label.

MUSHROOM TIPS

• Keep mushrooms white by cooking *à blanc* with lemon juice, salt and pepper and a little water.

• Use the soaking liquid from dried mushrooms to add flavor to sauces and stocks.

• Add dried mushrooms to fresh for extra flavor.

• Add a few mushrooms to stuffings, soups and stir-fries. Serve cooked mushrooms as a vegetable with meat, fish, poultry or game dishes.

• Always buy wild mushrooms from an authenticated source, and never pick and eat wild mushrooms unless they have been identified by an expert.

Appetizers and Snacks

Mushrooms add scented flavor to delicious snacks;

just simply served on toast, in a creamy soup, with a crisp

crunchy coating, stuffed with garlic butter, or

with sole as a splendid appetizer.

MUSHROOMS ON TOAST

Mushrooms have a happy relationship with garlic, but too often the intense flavor of the garlic takes over. The garlic here is tempered with a generous amount of fresh parsley and a touch of lemon.

Serves 4

2 tablespoons sweet butter, plus extra
   for spreading

1 onion, chopped

1 garlic clove, crushed

12 ounces assorted mushrooms, such as
   flat, crimini, and shiitake, trimmed
   and sliced

3 tablespoons dry sherry

5 tablespoons chopped fresh parsley

1 tablespoon lemon juice

4 slices brown or white bread

salt and ground black pepper

COOK'S TIP

Italian parsley has a good flavor and keeps well in the fridge. To keep it really fresh, stand it in a jar of water and cover with a plastic bag.

Melt the butter in a large nonstick frying pan, add the onion, and fry over low heat without letting it color.

Add the garlic and mushrooms, cover and cook for 3–5 minutes. Add the sherry and cook uncovered to evaporate the liquid.

Stir in the chopped fresh parsley and lemon juice, and then season to taste with salt and pepper.

Toast the bread and generously spread with butter. Serve immediately with the mushrooms spooned over the toast.

CRUNCHY MUSHROOMS WITH DILL DIP

These crisp bites are ideal as an informal appetizer or served with drinks.

Serves 4–6

2 cups fresh fine white bread crumbs

1½ tablespoons shredded sharp
   Cheddar cheese

1 teaspoon paprika

8 ounces flat mushrooms

2 egg whites

For the tomato and dill dip

4 ripe tomatoes

½ cup cottage cheese

4 tablespoons plain low-fat yogurt

1 garlic clove, crushed

2 tablespoons chopped fresh dill

salt and ground black pepper

dill sprig, to garnish

Preheat the oven to 375°F. Mix the bread crumbs, cheese and paprika together in a bowl.

Wipe the mushrooms clean and trim the stalks, if necessary. Lightly whisk the egg whites with a fork until frothy.

Dip each mushroom into the egg whites, then into the bread crumb mixture. Repeat until all the mushrooms are coated.

Place the mushrooms on a nonstick baking sheet. Bake in the preheated oven for 15 minutes, or until tender and the coating has turned golden and crunchy.

To make the dip, score the bases of the tomatoes and plunge them into a saucepan of boiling water for 1 minute, then into a saucepan of cold water. Slip off the skins. Halve the tomatoes, remove the seeds and cores, and roughly chop the flesh.

Put the cottage cheese, yogurt, garlic clove, and dill into a mixing bowl and stir to combine thoroughly. Season to taste with salt and black pepper. Add the chopped tomatoes and stir to combine. Spoon the mixture into a serving dish and garnish with a sprig of fresh dill. Serve the mushrooms hot, together with the dip.

STUFFED MUSHROOMS

These mushrooms are perfect for dinner parties, or serve them in larger portions as a light supper dish.

Serves 4

12 ounces large flat mushrooms,
*   stems removed*

3 garlic cloves, crushed

¾ cup butter, softened

3 cups fresh white bread crumbs

1 cup chopped fresh parsley

1 egg, beaten

salt and cayenne pepper

8 cherry tomatoes, to garnish

Preheat the oven to 375°F. Arrange the mushrooms cup-side uppermost on a baking sheet. Mix together the crushed garlic and butter in a small bowl and divide ½ cup of the butter among the mushrooms.

Melt the remaining butter in a large, nonstick frying pan, add the bread crumbs and lightly fry until golden brown. Place the chopped parsley in a bowl, add the bread crumbs, season to taste with salt and pepper and mix to combine well.

Stir in the egg and use the mixture to fill the mushroom caps. Bake for 10–15 minutes until the topping has browned and the mushrooms have softened. Serve garnished with the tomatoes cut into quarters.

COOK'S TIP
If you are planning ahead,
stuffed mushrooms can be
prepared up to 12 hours in
advance and kept in the fridge
before baking.

MUSHROOM SOUP

The crimini mushrooms give additional flavor to this delicious mixed mushroom soup.

Serves 4

4 tablespoons sweet butter

4 shallots or 1 onion, chopped

8 ounces closed cup mushrooms,
*   trimmed and chopped*

1 garlic clove, crushed

3¾ cups homemade or canned chicken
*   broth, boiling*

6 ounces crimini mushrooms, trimmed
*   and sliced*

4 tablespoons heavy cream

2 tablespoons lemon juice

salt and ground black pepper

3 tablespoons chopped fresh parsley,
*   to garnish*

crusty bread, to serve

M elt half of the butter in a saucepan, add the shallots or onion, and cook gently without letting them color. Add the cup mushrooms and garlic, and sauté until the mushrooms soften and the juices begin to run. Add the chicken broth, bring back to a boil and simmer for 15 minutes. Place in a food processor or blender, and process until smooth. Return to the pan.

Melt the remaining butter in a nonstick frying pan, add the crimini mushrooms and gently fry over low heat without letting them color. Add to the saucepan and simmer for a further minute.

Stir in the cream, and add lemon juice and salt and pepper to taste. Serve ladled into four warmed soup bowls, sprinkled with parsley and accompanied by crusty fresh bread.

ENGLISH MUFFINS WITH MUSHROOMS

English muffins, frozen spinach, and a few mushrooms form the base for this satisfying snack. Any flatfish will do, although sole works best of all.

Serves 2

½ cup butter, plus extra for
*   buttering muffins*
1 onion, chopped
4 ounces crimini mushrooms, sliced
2 fresh thyme sprigs, chopped
10 ounces frozen leaf spinach, thawed
3 pounds sole or flounder to yield
*   1½ pounds skinned fillet*
2 white English muffins, split
4 tablespoons crème fraîche or
*   heavy cream*
salt and ground black pepper

Heat 4 tablespoons of the butter in a saucepan, add the chopped onion, and gently cook over low heat until softened but without letting it color at all.

Add the mushrooms and thyme, cover and cook for 2–3 minutes more. Remove the lid and increase the heat to drive off any excess moisture.

Using the back of a large spoon, press the thawed frozen spinach in a strainer to squeeze out all the liquid.

Heat a further 2 tablespoons of the butter in a saucepan, add the spinach, heat through, and season to taste.

Melt the remaining butter in a large frying pan, season the sole or flounder fillets and, with skin side uppermost, cook for 2 minutes, then turn and cook for 2 minutes more.

Toast and butter the muffins. To serve, divide the fillets among them, top with spinach and a layer of mushrooms, then finish with a spoonful of crème fraîche or heavy cream.

COOK'S TIP
Approximately half of the weight of flatfish is bone, so if buying your fish whole, ask the fishmonger to give you enough for the correct weight of boned fish.

Fish and Shellfish

Seafood and shiitake, oyster and crimini mushrooms

make perfect partners in a fine selection of flavorful

dishes, whether served as a sauce with salmon,

with seafood in a savory pilaf, or Japanese-style

in tuna teriyaki.

TROUT WITH MUSHROOM SAUCE

The subtle flavor of trout is enhanced by this creamy mushroom sauce.

Serves 4

8 pink trout fillets

seasoned flour, for dusting

6 tablespoons butter

1 garlic clove, chopped

2 teaspoons chopped fresh sage

12 ounces assorted mushrooms, such as
*   button, crimini and oyster, trimmed*
*   and sliced*

6 tablespoons dry white wine

1 cup heavy cream

salt and ground black pepper

sage sprigs, to garnish

Remove the skin from the trout fillets, then carefully remove any bones. Lightly dust the trout fillets on both sides in the seasoned flour, shaking off any excess.

Melt the butter in a large frying pan, add the trout fillets and fry gently over moderate heat for 4–5 minutes, turning once. Remove from the pan and keep warm. Add the chopped garlic, sage, and mushrooms to the pan and gently fry until softened.

Pour in the wine and boil briskly to allow the alcohol to evaporate. Stir in the cream and season to taste with salt and pepper.

Serve the trout fillets on warmed plates with the sauce spooned over. Garnish with a few sage sprigs.

COOK'S TIP

Use a large sharp knife to ease
the skin from the trout fillets,
then pull out any bones from the
flesh – a pair of tweezers makes
easy work of this fiddly task!

SALMON WITH TARRAGON AND MUSHROOMS

Tarragon has a distinctive aniseed flavor that is good with fish, cream, and mushrooms. This recipe uses a selection of mushrooms to provide both texture and flavor.

Serves 4

4 tablespoons sweet butter

4 × 6-ounce salmon steaks

1 shallot, finely chopped

*6 ounces assorted mushrooms, such as
   oyster, shiitake, cèpes, and morels,
   trimmed and sliced*

⅞ cup chicken or vegetable broth

2 teaspoons cornstarch

½ teaspoon mustard

3½ tablespoons sour cream

3 tablespoons chopped fresh tarragon

1 teaspoon white wine vinegar

salt and cayenne pepper

new potatoes and green salad, to serve

Melt half of the butter in a large, nonstick frying pan, season the salmon, and cook over moderate heat for 8 minutes, turning once. Transfer to a plate, cover, and keep warm.

Melt the remaining butter in the pan, add the shallot, and gently cook over low heat without letting it color. Add the mushrooms and continue to cook until the juices begin to flow. Add the chicken or vegetable broth and simmer for a further 2–3 minutes.

Put the cornstarch and mustard in a cup and blend with 1 tablespoon of water. Stir into the mushroom mixture and bring to a simmer, stirring continuously, to thicken. Add the cream, chopped fresh tarragon, vinegar, and more seasoning.

If you like, remove the skin from the salmon steaks: insert a fork between the flesh and skin and wind the skin around the fork in a fluent action. Spoon the mushrooms over each salmon steak and serve with new potatoes and a green salad.

COOK'S TIP
*Fresh tarragon will bruise and
darken after chopping, so chop
just before you need it.*

SEAFOOD AND MUSHROOM PILAF

This all-in-one-pan main course is a satisfying meal for any day of the week. For a special meal,
substitute dry white wine for the orange juice.

Serves 4

2 teaspoons olive oil

generous 1 cup long grain rice

1 teaspoon ground turmeric

1 red bell pepper, seeded and diced

1 small onion, finely chopped

2 zucchini, sliced

5 ounces flat mushrooms, halved

1½ cups fish or chicken broth

⅔ cup orange juice

12 ounces whitefish fillets

12 fresh mussels in the shell, or cooked,
   shelled mussels

salt and ground black pepper

grated rind of 1 orange, to garnish

Heat the oil in a large, nonstick frying pan, add the rice and turmeric and sauté over low heat for about 1 minute.

Add the bell pepper, onion, zucchini, and mushrooms. Stir in the broth and orange juice. Bring to a boil.

Reduce the heat and add the fish. Cover and simmer gently for about 15 minutes, until the rice is tender and the liquid absorbed. Stir in the mussels and heat thoroughly. Adjust the seasoning to taste and garnish with the grated orange rind. Serve immediately.

FISH BALLS IN MUSHROOM SAUCE

This quick meal is a good choice for young children, as you can guarantee no bones.

Serves 4

*1 pound whitefish fillets such as cod or
flounder, skinned*

*4 tablespoons fresh whole wheat
bread crumbs*

*2 tablespoons snipped fresh chives
or finely chopped scallions*

14-ounce can chopped tomatoes

2 ounces flat mushrooms, sliced

salt and ground black pepper

snipped fresh chives, to garnish

snow peas, to serve

COOK'S TIP

*Instead of using a can of
chopped tomatoes and fresh
mushrooms, you could substitute
a jar of ready-made tomato and
mushroom sauce. Just add the
fish balls and simmer gently for
10 minutes.*

Cut the fish fillets into large chunks and place in a food processor. Add the whole wheat bread crumbs and snipped chives or chopped scallions. Season to taste with salt and black pepper, and process until the fish is finely chopped but still has some texture left.

Divide the fish mixture into about 16 even-size pieces, then shape them into balls with your hands.

Place the tomatoes and mushrooms in a wide saucepan and cook over moderate heat until boiling. Add the fish balls, cover, and simmer for about 10 minutes until cooked. Serve hot garnished with snipped fresh chives and accompanied by snow peas.

TUNA SHIITAKE TERIYAKI

Teriyaki is a sweet soy marinade usually used to glaze meat. Here teriyaki enhances fresh tuna steaks served with rich shiitake mushrooms.

Serves 4

4 × 6-ounce fresh tuna or yellow
  tail steaks
pinch of salt
6 ounces shiitake mushrooms, sliced
²/₃ cup teriyaki sauce
8 ounces white radish, peeled
2 large carrots, peeled
plain boiled rice, to serve

Place the tuna or yellow tail steaks in a shallow dish and season them with a sprinkling of salt, then set aside for about 20 minutes for the salt to penetrate. Add the sliced mushrooms to the dish and pour the teriyaki sauce over the fish steaks and mushrooms. Leave to marinate for about 20–30 minutes more or for longer if you have the time.

Preheat a moderate broiler or barbecue grill. Remove the tuna or yellow tail steaks from the marinade and reserve the marinade. Broil or barbecue the fish for 8 minutes, turning once.

Transfer the mushrooms and marinade to a stainless steel saucepan and simmer for about 3–4 minutes.

Slice the white radish and carrots thinly, then shred the vegetables finely with a chopping knife. Arrange a heap of each on four serving plates and add the fish steaks, with the mushrooms and sauce poured over. Serve at once with plain boiled rice.

COOK'S TIP

One of the finest teriyaki sauces is made by the company Kikkoman and can be found in most large supermarkets.

Meat and Poultry

Superbly creamy stroganoff; fricassée with rich woodland flavors; aromatic, herbed rösti; tender beef in wine with a crisp pastry topping; wild mushroom braid and a delectable filet mignon are some of the delights on offer.

BEEF AND MUSHROOM STROGANOFF

A version of the classic recipe for stroganoff, made with fillet steak, wild mushrooms, and cream.

Serves 4

1 pound fillet steak, trimmed and cut
*   into thin strips*

2 tablespoons olive oil

3 tablespoons brandy

2 shallots, finely chopped

8 ounces oyster mushrooms, trimmed
*   and halved*

²⁄₃ cup beef broth

5 tablespoons sour cream

1 teaspoon Dijon mustard

¹⁄₂ sweet cornichon, chopped

3 tablespoons chopped fresh parsley

salt and ground black pepper

buttered noodles and poppy seeds,
*   to serve*

COOK'S TIP
If you don't want to go to the
expense of buying fillet steak,
choose either best rump or
sirloin instead.

Season the steak with pepper. Heat half of the oil in a large, heavy-based frying pan and cook for 2 minutes. Transfer the meat to a plate.

Place the frying pan over moderately high heat and brown the sediment. Stand back from the pan, add the brandy, tilt toward the flame (or ignite with a match if cooking on an electric stove top) and burn off the alcohol vapor. Pour these juices over the meat, cover, and keep warm.

Wipe the pan clean. Heat the remaining oil, add the shallots and fry until lightly brown. Add the mushrooms and cook for 3–4 minutes to soften.

Pour over the broth and simmer for a few minutes more and then add the sour cream, mustard, and cornichon together with the steak and its juices. Simmer briefly, season to taste with salt and pepper, and stir in the chopped parsley. Serve with buttered noodles garnished with poppy seeds.

CHICKEN AND MUSHROOM FRICASSEE

A fricassée is a light stew, here accompanied by a sauce with a rich woodland flavor.

Serves 4

3 × 4-ounce chicken breasts, sliced

4 ounces smoked rindless bacon,
*   cut into pieces*

4 tablespoons sweet butter

1 tablespoon vegetable oil

5 tablespoons dry sherry or white wine

1 onion, chopped

12 ounces assorted mushrooms, such as
*   cèpes, closed button, and oyster,*
*   trimmed and sliced*

3 tablespoons flour

2¼ cups chicken broth

2 teaspoons lemon juice

4 tablespoons chopped fresh parsley

salt and ground black pepper

plain boiled rice, carrots, and baby
*   corn, to serve*

In a flameproof casserole, brown the chicken and bacon in half of the butter and the oil. Place in a shallow dish and pour off any excess fat.

Return the casserole to the heat and brown the residue. Pour in the sherry or wine and stir with a flat wooden spoon to deglaze the pan. Pour the liquid over the chicken and wipe the casserole clean.

Sauté the onion in the remaining butter until golden brown. Add the mushrooms and cook, stirring frequently, for about 6–8 minutes or until their juices begin to run. Stir in the flour, then remove the pan from the heat. Gradually add the chicken broth and stir well until the flour is absorbed.

Add the chicken and bacon with the juices, return to the heat and stir to thicken. Simmer for 10–15 minutes and then add the lemon juice, parsley, and seasoning. Serve with plain boiled rice, carrots, and baby corn.

MUSHROOM ROSTI WITH BACON

Dried cèpes or porcini mushrooms, commonly found in Italian delicatessens, are a good substitute for fresh.

Serves 4

1½ pounds baking potatoes, peeled

¼ ounce dried cèpes or porcini

2 fresh thyme sprigs, chopped

2 tablespoons chopped fresh parsley

4 tablespoons vegetable oil, for frying

4 × 4-ounce unsmoked bacon slices

pinch of salt

4 eggs, to serve

1 bunch watercress, to serve

COOK'S TIP

A large rösti can be made in a nonstick frying pan. Allow 12 minutes to cook. Halfway through the cooking time, invert the rösti onto a large plate and slide back into the pan.

Bring the potatoes to a boil in a large saucepan of salted water and cook for 5 minutes. Meanwhile, cover the mushrooms with boiling water to soften. Drain, then chop them roughly.

Drain the potatoes, allow them to cool and shred them coarsely. Add the mushrooms, thyme, and parsley and mix together well.

Heat 2 tablespoons of the oil in a frying pan, spoon in the rösti mixture in heaps and flatten. Fry for 6 minutes, turning once during cooking.

Preheat a moderate broiler and cook the bacon slices until sizzling. Heat the remaining oil in a frying pan and fry the eggs as you like them. Serve the rösti together with the eggs and bacon and the watercress.

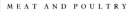

STEAK AND MUSHROOM PIE

Tender chunks of beef are cooked in a rich mushroom and wine sauce. The crisp filo pastry crust makes a change from the more traditional shortcrust or puff pastry topping.

Serves 4

1 onion, finely chopped

¾ cup beef broth

1 pound lean sirloin or top round steak,
   cut into 1-inch cubes

½ cup dry red wine

3 tablespoons flour

8 ounces button mushrooms, halved

5 sheets filo pastry

2 teaspoons sunflower oil

salt and ground black pepper

mashed potatoes and wax beans,
   to serve

Simmer the onion with ½ cup of the broth in a large, covered, nonstick saucepan for 5 minutes. Uncover and continue to cook, stirring occasionally, until the broth has reduced entirely. Transfer the onion to a plate and set aside until required.

Add the steak to the saucepan and dry-fry until the meat is lightly browned. Return the onion to the saucepan together with the remaining broth and the red wine. Cover and simmer gently for about 1½ hours, or until the meat is tender.

Preheat the oven to 375°F. Blend the flour with 3 tablespoons of cold water, add to the saucepan and continue to simmer, stirring all the time, until the sauce has thickened.

Add the mushrooms and continue to cook for 3 minutes. Season to taste with salt and pepper and spoon into a 5 cup pie dish.

Brush a sheet of filo pastry with a little of the sunflower oil, then crumple it up loosely and place oil-side up over the filling. Repeat with the remaining sheets of pastry and oil.

Bake in the oven for about 25–30 minutes until the pastry is golden brown and crispy. Serve with creamy mashed potatoes and freshly cooked wax beans.

SAUSAGE AND MUSHROOM BRAID PUFF

Fresh pork sausages needn't be cooked in their casings. To make the most of them, remove the meat and wrap it in a puff pastry package. A thick seam of wild mushrooms is a delicious addition.

Serves 4

4 tablespoons sweet butter

½ garlic clove, crushed

1 tablespoon chopped fresh thyme

1 pound assorted mushrooms, such as cèpes, oyster, and flat, trimmed and sliced

1 cup fresh white bread crumbs

5 tablespoons chopped fresh parsley

12 ounces puff pastry, thawed if frozen

1½ pounds pork sausages

1 egg, beaten with a pinch of salt

salt and ground black pepper

Preheat the oven to 350°F. Heat the butter in a large, nonstick frying pan, add the crushed garlic, chopped thyme, and sliced mushrooms and sauté gently over low heat for 5–6 minutes until soft, but not browned. When the mushroom juices begin to run, increase the heat to evaporate the juices. When dry, stir in the bread crumbs and chopped parsley and season well with salt and black pepper.

Roll the pastry out on a floured surface to form a 14- × 10-inch rectangle and place on a large ungreased baking sheet.

Remove the casings from the sausages and discard. Place half of the sausage meat in a 5-inch strip along the center of the pastry. Cover with the mushroom mixture, then put another layer of sausage meat over the mushrooms.

Make a series of 1-inch slanting cuts in the pastry on each side of the filling. Fold the two ends of pastry over the filling, moisten the pastry with beaten egg, and then cross the top with alternate strips of pastry from each side. Allow to rest for 40 minutes, brush with a little more egg, and bake in the oven for 1 hour. Serve immediately.

COOK'S TIP

A good pinch of salt added to a beaten egg will break it down and improve the finished glaze.

FILET MIGNON WITH MUSHROOMS

Large mushroom caps are readily available and look attractive especially when they are fluted as in this dish.

Serves 4

4 thin slices white bread

4 ounces pâté de foie gras *or* mousse
   de foie gras

4 closed cup mushrooms

5 tablespoons butter

2 teaspoons vegetable oil

4 fillet steaks (about 1 inch thick)

3–4 tablespoons Madeira or port

½ cup beef broth

bunch of watercress, to garnish

Cut the bread into rounds about the same diameter as the steaks, using a large round cutter or by cutting into squares, then cutting off the corners with a sharp knife. Toast the bread and spread with the *foie gras* or *mousse de foie gras*, dividing it evenly. Place the croûtons on warmed plates.

Flute the mushrooms using a small, sharp knife, if you wish, for a decorative effect. Melt 2 tablespoons of the butter in a nonstick frying pan, add the mushrooms, and sauté over moderate heat until golden. Transfer to a plate and keep warm until required.

In the same pan, melt another 2 tablespoons of the butter with the oil over moderately high heat, swirling to combine. When the butter begins to brown, add the steaks and cook for about 6–8 minutes, turning once, until cooked as preferred (medium-rare meat will still be slightly soft when pressed, medium will be springy, and well-done firm). Place the steaks on top of the croûtons and top with the mushrooms.

Add the Madeira or port to the pan and boil for 20–30 seconds. Add the broth and boil over high heat until reduced by three-quarters, then swirl in the remaining butter. To serve, pour a little sauce over each steak, then garnish with watercress.

COOK'S TIP

If pâté de foie gras *is difficult to find, you could substitute pork liver pâté in this recipe.*

Pasta and Rice

Mushrooms add their delicate flavor to all sorts of

pasta and rice dishes. With the addition of herbs, nuts,

cheese, bacon and fresh vegetables, they enhance

stir-fries, risottos, pasta sauces, bakes and rice salads.

SPAGHETTI WITH MUSHROOM SAUCE

The combination of mixed mushrooms and freshly chopped sweet basil tossed with spaghetti would be well complemented by a fresh tomato salad.

Serves 4

4 tablespoons butter

1 onion, chopped

12 ounces spaghetti

12 ounces assorted mushrooms, such as crimini and flat, sliced

1 garlic clove, chopped

1¼ cups sour cream

2 tablespoons chopped fresh basil

4 tablespoons shredded Parmesan cheese

salt and ground black pepper

torn Italian parsley, to garnish

grated Parmesan cheese, to serve

Melt the butter in a large, nonstick frying pan, add the onion, and fry over moderate heat until softened. Meanwhile, cook the pasta following the instructions on the package.

Stir the sliced mushrooms and chopped garlic into the onion mixture and fry for 10 minutes more, until softened.

Add the sour cream, basil, and Parmesan cheese, and season to taste with salt and pepper. Cover and heat through.

Drain the pasta thoroughly and toss it with the sauce. Garnish with torn Italian parsley. Serve immediately, with plenty of Parmesan cheese.

PASTA WITH MUSHROOMS AND CHORIZO

The delicious combination of mushrooms and spicy sausage makes this a tempting supper dish.

Serves 4

4 tablespoons olive oil

1 garlic clove, chopped

1 celery stalk, chopped

12 ounces pasta twists

8 ounces chorizo sausage, sliced

8 ounces assorted mushrooms,
  such as oyster, crimini,
  and shiitake

1 tablespoon lemon juice

2 tablespoons chopped fresh oregano

salt and ground black pepper

finely chopped fresh parsley, to garnish

Heat the oil in a large, nonstick frying pan, add the garlic and celery, and cook over moderate heat until softened. Meanwhile, cook the pasta following the instructions on the package. When cooked, strain and keep warm until required.

Add the chorizo sausage to the garlic and celery and cook for 5 minutes more, stirring occasionally until browned.

Add the mushrooms and cook for 4 minutes more, stirring occasionally until slightly softened. Stir in the remaining ingredients, except the garnish, and cook until heated through.

Add the pasta twists to the pan and toss thoroughly with the mushroom and chorizo sausage mixture until well combined. Serve immediately, garnished with the finely chopped fresh parsley.

COOK'S TIP

This dish is delicious served with lots of Parmesan cheese shavings. Use any combination of mushrooms you like for this flavorful sauce.

NUTTY RICE AND MUSHROOM STIR-FRY

This delicious and substantial supper dish can be eaten hot or cold accompanied by different salads.

Serves 4–6

12 ounces long grain rice

3 tablespoons sunflower oil

1 small onion, roughly chopped

8 ounces flat mushrooms, sliced

½ cup hazelnuts, roughly chopped

½ cup pecans, roughly chopped

½ cup almonds, roughly chopped

4 tablespoons chopped fresh parsley

salt and ground black pepper

Rinse the rice, then cook for about 10–12 minutes in 2½–3 cups water in a saucepan with a tight-fitting lid. When cooked, refresh under cold water. Heat a wok, then add half of the oil. Heat the oil and when hot, stir-fry the rice for 2–3 minutes. Remove and set aside until required.

Add the remaining oil and stir-fry the onion for 2 minutes more, until softened. Mix in the flat mushrooms and stir-fry for 2 minutes more.

Add all the nuts and stir-fry for 1 minute. Return the rice to the wok and stir-fry for about 3 minutes. Season to taste. To serve, stir in the parsley.

MUSHROOM MACARONI AND CHEESE

Macaroni and cheese is an all-time classic from the mid-week menu. Here it is served in a light creamy sauce with mushrooms and topped with pine nuts.

Serves 4

1 pound quick-cooking elbow macaroni

3 tablespoons olive oil

8 ounces flat mushrooms, sliced

2 fresh thyme sprigs

4 tablespoons flour

1 vegetable bouillon cube, crumbled

2¹/₂ cups milk

¹/₂ teaspoon celery salt

1 teaspoon Dijon mustard

1¹/₂ cups shredded Cheddar cheese

2 tablespoons grated
  Parmesan cheese

¹/₄ cup pine nuts

salt and ground black pepper

Cook the macaroni following the instructions on the package. Heat the oil in a heavy-based saucepan, add the mushrooms and thyme, cover, and cook over low heat for 2–3 minutes. Stir in the flour and remove from the heat, add the bouillon cube and stir continuously until evenly blended. Add the milk a little at a time, stirring after each addition. Add the celery salt, mustard, and Cheddar cheese, and season to taste with salt and pepper. Stir and simmer briefly for 1–2 minutes until thickened.

Preheat the broiler. Drain the pasta, toss into the sauce and fill four individual dishes or one large flameproof baking dish. Sprinkle with Parmesan cheese and pine nuts; broil until brown and bubbly. Serve immediately.

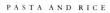

MUSHROOM AND BACON RISOTTO

Mixed mushrooms and smoked bacon add savory flavor to this classic risotto.

Serves 4

2 tablespoons sunflower oil

1 large onion, chopped

3 ounces smoked bacon, chopped

12 ounces arborio or risotto rice

1–2 garlic cloves, crushed

½ cup dried sliced mushrooms, soaked in a little boiling water

6 ounces asssorted mushrooms, such as button and crimini

5 cups hot broth

a few sprigs of oregano or thyme

1 tablespoon butter

a little dry white wine

3 tablespoons chopped, peeled tomato

8–10 black olives, pitted and quartered

salt and ground black pepper

thyme sprigs, to garnish

Heat the oil in a large, heavy-based pan with a lid. Gently cook the onion and bacon until the onion is tender and the bacon fat has run out.

Stir in the rice and garlic and cook over high heat for 2–3 minutes until the rice is well coated. Add the dried mushrooms and their liquid, the fresh mushrooms and half of the broth, the oregano, and season to taste. Bring gently to a boil, then reduce the heat. Cover tightly and leave to cook.

Gently stir the risotto. If quite dry, slowly add more liquid. (Don't stir too often, as this lets the steam and flavor out.) Add more liquid as required until the rice is cooked, but not mushy.

Just before serving, stir in the butter, white wine, tomato, and olives and taste for seasoning. Serve hot, garnished with thyme sprigs.

MUSHROOMS WITH WILD RICE

Broiling brings out the flavor of the summer vegetables in this recipe.

Serves 4

scant ¹/₂ cup wild rice

scant ¹/₂ cup long grain rice

1 large eggplant, thickly sliced

1 red, 1 yellow, and 1 green bell
  pepper, seeded and cut into quarters

2 red onions, sliced

8 ounces crimini or shiitake mushrooms

2 small zucchini, cut in half lengthwise

olive oil, for brushing

For the dressing

6 tablespoons extra virgin olive oil

2 tablespoons balsamic vinegar

2 garlic cloves, crushed

salt and ground black pepper

Put the wild rice in a saucepan of cold salted water. Bring to a boil, then reduce the heat, cover, and cook gently for 40 minutes, before adding the long grain rice. Cook for 10 minutes more, or until the grains are tender.

For the dressing, mix all the ingredients in a screw-top jar. Then arrange the vegetables on a broiling rack, brush with olive oil and broil for 8–10 minutes, until tender and well browned, turning them occasionally and brushing again with oil.

Drain the rice and toss in half of the dressing. Tip into a serving dish and arrange the broiled vegetables on top. Pour over the remaining dressing and serve immediately.

Vegetable Dishes

A variety of wild and cultivated mushrooms demonstrate
their amazing versatility in a diverse array of recipes,
from bean dishes to burgers, roulades to ragoûts,
pizza to pies, and from strudel to sautées and soufflés.

MIXED MUSHROOM RAGOUT

These mushrooms are delicious served hot or cold and can be prepared up to two days in advance.

Serves 4

1 small onion, finely chopped

1 garlic clove, crushed

1 teaspoon coriander seeds, crushed

2 tablespoons red wine vinegar

1 tablespoon soy sauce

1 tablespoon dry sherry

2 teaspoons tomato paste

2 teaspoons light brown sugar

⅔ cup vegetable broth

4 ounces small flat mushrooms

4 ounces crimini mushrooms, quartered

4 ounces oyster mushrooms, sliced

salt and ground black pepper

cilantro sprig, to garnish

Put the first nine ingredients into a large, heavy-based saucepan. Bring to a boil and reduce the heat. Cover and simmer for 5 minutes.

Uncover the saucepan and simmer for 5 minutes more, or until the liquid has reduced by half.

Add the small flat and crimini mushrooms and simmer for 3 minutes more. Stir in the oyster mushrooms and cook for 2 minutes more.

Remove the mushrooms with a slotted spoon and transfer them to a serving dish. Boil the juices for about 5 minutes, or until reduced to about 5 tablespoons. Season to taste with salt and pepper.

Allow the juices to cool for 2–3 minutes, then pour over the mushrooms. Serve hot or well chilled, garnished with a sprig of fresh cilantro.

49

MUSHROOM TART

The region of Alsace in France is renowned for its abundance of wild mushrooms. This tart is good with a cool Alsatian wine. Serve with baked potatoes and a mixed salad, if you like.

Serves 4

*12 ounces unsweetened pie pastry,
   thawed if frozen*

4 tablespoons sweet butter

3 onions, halved and sliced

*12 ounces assorted mushrooms, such
   as cèpes, morels, oyster, and flat*

1 thyme sprig, chopped

pinch of grated nutmeg

3 1/2 tablespoons whole milk

3 1/2 tablespoons light cream

1 egg and 2 egg yolks

salt and ground black pepper

Preheat the oven to 375°F and lightly grease a 9-inch loose-based cake or quiche pan with butter. Roll out the pastry on a lightly floured board and line the pan. Rest the pastry in the fridge for 1 hour.

Place three squares of wax paper in the tart crust, fill with rice or baking beans and bake for 25 minutes. Lift out the paper and rice or beans and leave to cool.

Melt the butter in a large, nonstick frying pan, add the onions, cover and cook slowly for 20 minutes. Add the mushrooms and thyme, and continue cooking for a further 10 minutes. Season to taste with the salt and pepper. Add the nutmeg.

Pour the milk and cream into a bowl and beat in the egg and egg yolks. Place the mushroom mixture in the crust and then pour over the milk and egg mixture. Bake for 15–20 minutes until the center is firm to the touch. Serve hot or let cool to room temperature.

COOK'S TIP

*To prepare ahead, the crust can
be partially baked and the filling
made in advance.*

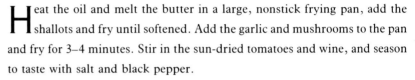

BEANS WITH MUSHROOMS

The mixture of mushrooms in this dish helps to give it a wonderfully rich and nutty flavor.

Serves 4

2 tablespoons olive oil

4 tablespoons butter

2 shallots, chopped

2–3 garlic cloves, crushed

1½ pounds assorted mushrooms, such as button, crimini and oyster, thickly sliced

4 pieces sun-dried tomatoes in oil, drained and chopped

6 tablespoons dry white wine

15-ounce can red kidney, pinto, or borlotti beans, drained

3 tablespoons grated Parmesan cheese

2 tablespoons chopped fresh parsley

salt and ground black pepper

freshly cooked pappardelle pasta, to serve

Heat the oil and melt the butter in a large, nonstick frying pan, add the shallots and fry until softened. Add the garlic and mushrooms to the pan and fry for 3–4 minutes. Stir in the sun-dried tomatoes and wine, and season to taste with salt and black pepper.

Stir in the beans and cook for 5–6 minutes more, until most of the liquid has evaporated and the beans are warmed through.

Stir in the Parmesan cheese. Sprinkle with the chopped fresh parsley and serve immediately with pappardelle.

SAUTEED MUSHROOMS

This is a quick dish to prepare and makes an ideal accompaniment to all kinds of roasted and broiled meats. Use any combination of mushrooms you can find.

Serves 6

2 pounds assorted fresh mushrooms,
    such as morels, cèpes, oyster,
    or shiitake
2 tablespoons olive oil
2 tablespoons sweet butter
2 garlic cloves, finely chopped
3–4 shallots, finely chopped
3–4 tablespoons chopped fresh parsley,
    or a mixture of fresh herbs
salt and ground black pepper

Wash and carefully dry any very dirty mushrooms. Trim the stems and cut the mushrooms into quarters or slice if very large.

Heat the oil in a large, nonstick frying pan, add the butter and swirl to melt over moderate heat. Stir in the assorted mushrooms and cook them for 4–5 minutes until starting to brown.

Add the garlic and shallots and cook for 4–5 minutes more until the mushrooms are tender and any liquid given off has evaporated. Season to taste with salt and pepper, and stir in the parsley or mixed herbs.

MUSHROOM AND CHEESE SOUFFLE PIE

A sophisticated mushroom flan with a cheese soufflé topping. Serve hot with a cranberry relish.

Serves 8

2 cups flour

3/4 cup butter

1 cup grated Parmesan cheese

1 egg

1 tablespoon Dijon mustard

For the filling

2 tablespoons butter

1 onion, finely chopped

1–2 garlic cloves, crushed

12 ounces mushrooms, chopped

1 tablespoon chopped fresh parsley

1 cup fresh white bread crumbs

salt and ground black pepper

For the cheese topping

2 tablespoons butter

2 tablespoons flour

1 1/4 cups milk

2 tablespoons grated Parmesan cheese

3/4 cup shredded Cheddar cheese

1 egg, separated

To make the pastry, sift the flour into a bowl and rub in the butter until the mixture resembles fine bread crumbs. Stir in the Parmesan cheese. Beat the egg with 1 tablespoon water. Add to the flour mixture and bind to a soft pliable dough. Knead until smooth, wrap, and chill for 30 minutes.

To make the filling, melt the butter in a large, nonstick frying pan, add the onion, and cook over moderate heat until tender. Add the garlic and mushrooms and cook, uncovered, for 5 minutes, stirring occasionally. Increase the heat and drive off any liquid in the pan. Remove the pan from the heat and stir in the chopped fresh parsley, bread crumbs, and seasoning. Allow to cool.

Preheat a baking sheet in the oven at 375°F. Lightly grease a 9-inch loose-based cake pan. Roll the dough out on a lightly floured board and line the pan. Rest the dough in the fridge for 1 hour.

To make the cheese topping, melt the butter in a saucepan, stir in the flour, and cook over low heat for 2 minutes. Gradually blend in the milk. Bring to a boil to thicken, and simmer for 2–3 minutes. Remove the pan from the heat and stir in the Parmesan and Cheddar cheeses and the egg yolk, and season well. Beat until smooth. Whisk the egg white until it holds soft peaks; fold the egg white into the topping.

To assemble the pie, spread the Dijon mustard evenly over the base of the crust. Spoon in the mushroom filling and level the surface. Pour over the cheese topping and bake the pie on the hot baking sheet for 35–45 minutes until set and golden.

MUSHROOM AND CHEESE STRUDEL

Based on a traditional Russian dish called Koulibiac, *this makes a perfect vegetarian main course or an unusual accompaniment to cold leftover turkey or sliced ham.*

Serves 4

¾ cup long grain rice

2 tablespoons butter

1–2 leeks, thinly sliced

12 ounces mushrooms, sliced

2 cups shredded Swiss or
  Cheddar cheese

8 ounces feta cheese, cubed

2 tablespoons raisins

½ cup chopped almonds or
  hazelnuts, toasted

2 tablespoons chopped fresh parsley

10 ounce package frozen filo
  pastry, thawed

2 tablespoons olive oil

salt and ground black pepper

Cook the rice in boiling, salted water for 10–12 minutes, until tender. Drain, rinse under cold running water, and set aside. Melt the butter in a saucepan, add the leeks and mushrooms and cook over moderate heat for 5 minutes. Transfer to a bowl to cool.

Add the well-drained rice, the cheeses, raisins, toasted nuts, and parsley, and season to taste (be careful with the salt as the feta cheese is very salty).

Preheat the oven to 375°F. Unwrap the filo pastry. Cover it with a piece of plastic wrap and a damp dish towel while you work. Lay a sheet of filo pastry on a large piece of wax paper and brush it with oil. Lay a second sheet on the paper, overlapping the first by 1 inch. Arrange another sheet with its long side running at right angles to the long sides of the first two. Lay a fourth sheet in the same way, overlapping by 1 inch. Continue in this way, alternating the layers of two sheets so that the join between the two sheets runs in the opposite direction for each layer.

Place the filling along the center of the pastry and shape it neatly with your hands into a rectangle about 4 × 12 inches.

Fold the pastry over the filling and roll the strudel over, with the help of the wax paper, so that the join is hidden underneath.

Lift the strudel on to a greased baking sheet and tuck the edges under so that the filling does not leak out during cooking. Brush with oil and bake for 30–40 minutes, until golden and crisp. Let the strudel stand for 5 minutes before cutting into generous slices.

SPINACH AND MUSHROOM SOUFFLE

Mushrooms combine especially well with eggs and spinach in this sensational soufflé. Almost any combination of mushrooms can be used, although the firmer varieties provide the best texture.

Serves 4

8 ounces fresh spinach, washed, or
 4 ounces frozen chopped spinach
4 tablespoons sweet butter, plus extra
 for greasing
1 garlic clove, crushed
6 ounces assorted mushrooms, such as
 cèpes, oyster, and flat
1 cup milk
3 tablespoons flour
6 eggs, separated
pinch of grated nutmeg
2 tablespoons grated Parmesan cheese
salt and ground black pepper

COOK'S TIP

*The soufflé base can be prepared
up to 12 hours in advance and
reheated before the beaten egg
whites are folded in.*

Preheat the oven to 375°F. Steam the spinach over moderate heat for 3–4 minutes. Cool under running water, then drain. Press out as much liquid as you can with the back of a large spoon and chop finely. If using frozen spinach, defrost, then squeeze dry in the same way.

Melt the butter in a saucepan, add the garlic and mushrooms, and cook over moderate heat until softened. Turn up the heat until the juices have evaporated. When dry, add the spinach and transfer the mixture to a bowl. Cover and keep warm until required.

Measure 3 tablespoons of the milk into a bowl. Bring the remainder to a boil. Stir the flour and egg yolks into the cold milk and blend well. Stir the boiling milk into the egg and flour mixture, return to the pan, and simmer to thicken, stirring constantly. Add the spinach mixture. Season to taste with salt, pepper, and grated nutmeg.

Butter a 3¾-cup soufflé dish, paying particular attention to the sides. Sprinkle with a little of the Parmesan. Set aside.

Whisk the egg whites until stiff. Bring the spinach mixture back to a boil. Remove from the heat. Stir in a spoonful of beaten egg white, then fold the mixture into the remaining egg white. Turn into the soufflé dish, spread level, sprinkle with the remaining Parmesan, and bake in the oven for about 25 minutes until puffed and golden. Serve the soufflé immediately.

MUSHROOM BURGERS

Any kind of mushroom can be used in this popular dish.

Serves 4

*4 ounces closed cup mushrooms,
  finely chopped*

1 small onion, chopped

1 small zucchini, chopped

1 carrot, chopped

¼ cup unsalted peanuts or cashews

2 cups fresh bread crumbs

2 tablespoons chopped fresh parsley

1 teaspoon yeast extract

fine oatmeal or flour, for shaping

salt and ground black pepper

green salad, to serve

Cook the mushrooms in a nonstick frying pan without oil, stirring, for 8–10 minutes to remove all the moisture.

In a food processor, process the onion, zucchini, carrot, and nuts until beginning to bind together. Stir in the mushrooms, bread crumbs, parsley, and yeast extract, and season to taste with salt and pepper. With the oatmeal or flour, shape into four burgers. Chill in the fridge.

Cook the burgers in a nonstick frying pan with very little oil or under a hot broiler for 8–10 minutes, turning once, until the burgers are cooked and golden brown. Serve hot with a green salad.

COOK'S TIP

You can prepare these burgers up to a day before cooking. Arrange them on a plate or tray and cover with plastic wrap, then chill until ready to cook.

CHICKEN AND SHIITAKE PIZZA

The addition of shiitake mushrooms adds an earthy flavor to this colorful pizza, while fresh red chili
makes a fiery addition, which you may wish to omit.

Serves 3–4

3 tablespoons olive oil

12 ounces chicken breast fillets,
skinned and cut into thin strips

1 bunch scallions, sliced

1 fresh red chili, seeded and chopped

1 red bell pepper, seeded and cut into
thin strips

3 ounces shiitake mushrooms, wiped
and sliced

3–4 tablespoons chopped fresh cilantro

1 pizza base, about 10–12-inch
diameter

1 tablespoon chili oil

5 ounces mozzarella cheese

salt and ground black pepper

Preheat the oven to 425°F. Heat 2 tablespoons of the olive oil in a wok or large frying pan, add the chicken, scallions, chili, bell pepper, and mushrooms and stir-fry over high heat for 2–3 minutes until the chicken is firm but still slightly pink within. Season to taste with salt and pepper.

Pour off any excess oil, then set aside the chicken mixture to cool. Stir the chopped fresh cilantro into the chicken mixture. Brush the pizza base with the chili oil. Spoon over the chicken mixture and drizzle the remaining olive oil over.

Shred the mozzarella and sprinkle it over the pizza. Bake for 15–20 minutes until crisp and golden. Serve immediately.

SPINACH AND MUSHROOM ROULADE

An attractive and impressive dish that is surprisingly simple to prepare.

Serves 6–8

1 pound fresh spinach

1 tablespoon butter

4 eggs, separated

pinch of grated nutmeg

4 tablespoons shredded Cheddar cheese

salt and ground black pepper

For the filling

2 tablespoons butter

12 ounces flat mushrooms, chopped

4 tablespoons flour

⅔ cup milk

3 tablespoons heavy cream

2 tablespoons snipped fresh chives

Preheat the oven to 375°F. Line a 9- × 13-inch jelly roll pan with wax paper. Wash the spinach thoroughly and remove the tough stalks, then cook the wet leaves in a covered pan without extra water until just tender. Drain the spinach well in a colander, squeezing out all the excess moisture, and then chop finely.

Tip the spinach into a bowl, beat in the butter and egg yolks, and season with salt, pepper, and nutmeg. Whisk the egg whites until stiff and fold into the spinach mixture. Spread into the pan and sprinkle with half the cheese. Bake for 10–12 minutes until just firm.

To make the filling, melt the butter in a saucepan, add the mushrooms, and fry over moderate heat until softened. Stir in the flour and cook for 1 minute. Gradually add the milk, then bring to a boil, stirring until thickened. Simmer for a further 2–3 minutes. Remove from the heat and stir in the cream and chives.

Remove the cooked roulade from the oven and turn out on to a sheet of wax paper. Peel off the lining paper and spread the roulade evenly with the mushroom filling.

Roll up the roulade fairly tightly and transfer to an ovenproof dish. Sprinkle over the remaining cheese and return the roulade to the oven for about 4–5 minutes to melt the cheese. Serve at once, cut into slices.

INDEX

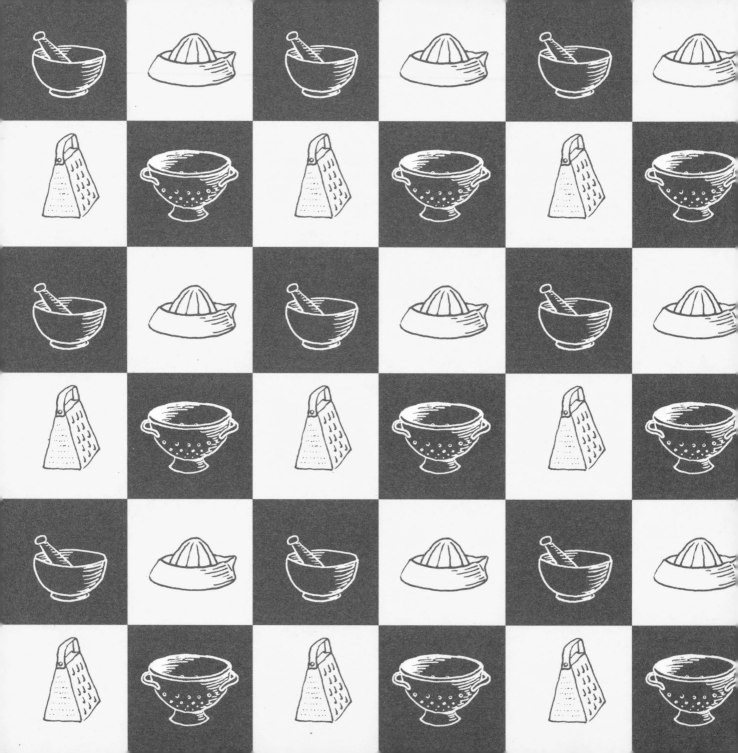